TAMIL NADU
TRAVEL GUIDE
2024

Tamil Nadu Treasures: Crafting Your Dream Vacation in 2024

INEZ M. MEDINA

TAMIL NADU TRAVEL GUIDE 2024

All Right Reserved!

No part of this book may be reproduced, stored in a retrieval system or transmitted in any form or by any, electronic or mechanical photocopying, recording or otherwise, without the prior written by the owner permission of the copyright owner

TABLE OF CONTENTS

INTRODUCTION

PLANNING YOUR TRIP

CHENNAI - Gateway to Tamil Nadu

SOUTHERN SPLENDORS - Madurai and Rameswaram

TRANQUIL COASTS - Coastal Towns and Beaches:

TEMPLE TRAILS - Thanjavur and Trichy

HILL STATIONS - Ooty and Kodaikanal

WILDLIFE ADVENTURES - Periyar National Park

CULTURAL EXPERIENCES - Music, Dance, and Arts:

EXPLORING TAMIL NADU ON A BUDGET: Unveiling Affordable Delights

CULINARY DELIGHTS OF TAMIL NADU: A Gastronomic Journey Through South Indian Flavors

PRACTICAL TRAVEL TIPS FOR EXPLORING TAMIL NADU: A Guide to Seamless Exploration

OFF THE BEATEN PATH IN TAMIL NADU: Discovering Hidden Gems

RESPONSIBLE TRAVEL IN TAMIL NADU: Nurturing Nature, Empowering Communities

TAMIL NADU TRAVEL GUIDE 2024

TAMIL NADU: A Tapestry of Experiences for Families and Solo Travelers

BEYOND TAMIL NADU: Exploring Nearby Destinations

CONCLUSION

EPILOGUE: Unveiling Hidden Legends - Untold Stories of Tamil Nadu

INTRODUCTION

Welcome to Tamil Nadu, a state in South India that skillfully combines historic customs with contemporary energy. Explore the rich historical tapestry, diverse cultures, and breathtaking landscapes of the Indian subcontinent as you travel across it with our 2024 travel guide.

Chennai, the capital of Tamil Nadu, is the entry point to a tale rich in history and breathtaking architecture. Prepare yourself for an immersion into religious ceremonies and the alluring smells of local foods as you trek through the southern marvels of Madurai and Rameswaram. Calm seaside villages like Tranquebar and Mahabalipuram entice visitors with stories of their maritime past and magnificent temples carved out of rock.

This book leads you through the foggy hill stations of Ooty and Kodaikanal in addition to revealing the architectural gems of Thanjavur and Trichy. Experience Periyar National Park's animal experiences first hand, and then feast on delicious food, dance, and music that showcase the many cultures there. Accompany us on a journey to uncover the undiscovered treasures, conscientious travel habits, and kinship warmth that characterize Tamil Nadu.

An Overview of Tamil Nadu

Located in southern India, Tamil Nadu is a region of captivating contrasts, where traditional customs and contemporary life live together. The state is famous for its varied landscapes, which span from lush plains to the scenic Nilgiri Hills and is bordered to the east by the Bay of Bengal. Tamil Nadu, the seventh-largest state in India, has a population that is as varied as its terrain and offers an intriguing fusion of urban sophistication and rural simplicity.

Historical Background

There is evidence that humans have lived in Tamil Nadu since ancient times, and the region's past is woven throughout Indian history. Through the Chola, Pandya, and Chera dynasties—each leaving an enduring imprint on the terrain—the region's illustrious history is revealed. Ancient temples like the Meenakshi Amman Temple in Madurai and the Brihadeeswarar Temple in Thanjavur are examples of architectural wonders that preserve the grandeur of the Chola period. The state's cultural mosaic has also been influenced by colonial influences, especially the British and the French, who left remnants of their presence in towns like Pondicherry and Chennai.

Cultural Diversity

The state of Tamil Nadu is home to a diverse range of customs that are treasured and handed down through the ages. The state is also known for its traditional arts, which are still very much in demand today. Examples of these include Bharatanatyam dance and Carnatic music. The calendar is punctuated by ornate and colorful holidays like Pongal, Diwali, and Navaratri, which provide tourists with a look into the vivid tapestry of Tamil culture. Being one of the oldest languages still in use, Tamil is proudly spoken. Language is a significant tool for expressing identity. The warmth and friendliness of the Tamil people provide the cultural experience a special twist by making guests feel not merely accepted but also embraced by the community.

Geography and Climate

Tamil Nadu has an astounding range of physical features, from lush plains to dry regions and thick forests. The state's 1,000 kilometers of coastline are home to immaculate beaches like Chennai's Marina Beach and the tranquil shores of Rameswaram. The lush hill stations of Ooty and Kodaikanal, which provide relief from the searing heat, are part of the Western Ghats, which beautify the western boundary.

Tamil Nadu's climate is as diverse as its terrain. The hill stations have a more temperate temperature year-round, whereas the coastal districts have a tropical environment with scorching summers and mild winters. The state's agricultural communities, which are the backbone of the economy, are sustained by the monsoon season, which runs from June to September. It offers respite to the parched regions and fills the rivers.

To sum up, Tamil Nadu is a symphony of geography, history, and culture that beckons visitors to discover its many facets of beauty. Tamil Nadu provides a diverse range of experiences that leave a lasting impression on those who explore its embrace, whether they are seeking the calm of ancient temples, the energy of cultural festivities, or the peace of hill getaways.

PLANNING YOUR TRIP

To guarantee a smooth and fulfilling trip, careful preparation is necessary before departing for Tamil Nadu. Everything from figuring out when to go to know the traditions of the area helps make your trip to this culturally rich and geographically varied state well-rounded.

Best Time to Visit:

Considering Tamil Nadu's climate fluctuations, the ideal time to visit is essential for a pleasurable trip. The best months to visit are those that occur between October and March when the temperature is lower and there is less precipitation. This period not only guarantees suitable touring in locations like Madurai, Chennai, and Ooty, but it also coincides with several festivals, enabling visitors to experience the lively cultural festivities that are an essential part of Tamil culture. If you like the monsoon, however, Tamil Nadu's beautiful landscapes spring to life from June to September. However, severe rains on occasion may interfere with outdoor activities.

Travel Essentials:

Packing necessities for your trip to Tamil Nadu might significantly impact how comfortable and enjoyable it is for you. Because of the warm weather, wear light, breezy clothes, but always bring layers, particularly if you want to visit the cooler hill areas. During daylight outings, suitable walking shoes, a wide-brimmed hat, and sunscreen are essential. Given the varied settings, it is advised to respect local traditions by dressing modestly when visiting temples in a blend of casual and formal attire.

It is essential to have a fully supplied travel medical pack that includes basic first aid supplies and any prescription drugs. Though the healthcare system in Tamil Nadu is well-developed, it's still a good idea to carry basic supplies like bug repellant and over-the-counter prescriptions for common illnesses so you're ready for any unforeseen medical issues. For your everyday trips, a reliable backpack, a reusable water bottle, and a power bank for your electronics are useful extras.

Visa and Entry criteria

It's important to know the criteria for both before you go to Tamil Nadu. To enter India, the majority of foreign visitors need a valid tourist visa. To ensure you have the most recent details on requirements and application processes for visas, it is recommended that you visit the Indian government's official website or get in touch with the Indian embassy or consulate in your country.

Make sure your passport is valid for at least six months after the date you want to go, and for convenience, carry both an electronic and hard duplicate of your passport and visa. Learn about the unique criteria for immigration into India, since they might change based on your nationality.

Health and Safety Advice:

You must follow sensible health and safety procedures while visiting Tamil Nadu. Even though the state offers a relatively safe atmosphere for visitors, it's advisable to exercise care. To stay hydrated, especially in the hot months, drink filtered or bottled water. Steer clear of undercooked or uncooked food, and give priority to eating at recognized restaurants.

See your healthcare physician well in advance to discuss any required immunizations or vaccines, since they may depend on your past travel experiences. Keep a modest medical kit with you at all times, filled with necessities like painkillers, antidiarrheal medicine, and any prescription drugs you may need. It is very recommended that you get travel insurance, which will cover medical emergencies and any cancellations.

Use care while crossing busy streets, obey traffic laws, and use dependable transit options. Keep an eye out for small-time theft in crowded places, particularly in busy marketplaces and popular tourist destinations.

Local Customs and Etiquette

To guarantee a good and culturally intensive trip to Tamil Nadu, it is important to respect local traditions and etiquette. Tamil Nadu residents are renowned for their gracious hospitality and devotion to customs. Wear modest clothing, covering your knees and shoulders, when you attend temples and other places of worship. It's traditional to take off your shoes before entering a temple, and it's wise to pay attention to local customs and follow their example in these hallowed places.

Because Tamil Nadu is home to a diverse range of cultures and rituals, it is polite to get permission before taking pictures of people or religious events. A customary "**Namaste**" with folded hands is often exchanged during greetings as a sign of respect.

Even though most people speak English, knowing a few simple Tamil words can improve your relationships and demonstrate that you appreciate the way of life here. It is normal to use both hands to receive meals and presents, and showing thanks is a highly regarded ritual.

To sum up, careful preparation is essential to having a rewarding vacation in Tamil Nadu. You can ensure that your trip to this fascinating state is enjoyable and fulfilling by researching the ideal time to visit, packing necessary goods, learning about visa procedures, putting health and safety first, and embracing local traditions.

CHENNAI - Gateway to Tamil Nadu

The dynamic entryway to the cultural, historical, and economic richness of Tamil Nadu is Chennai, the state capital, which lies tucked away along the Coromandel Coast. Chennai captures the spirit of Tamil Nadu's many offers, from its busy streets to its tranquil beaches.

Exploring the Capital City

Chennai is a vast city that skillfully blends technology and history. Because of its booming car sector, Chennai is often referred to as the "**Detroit of India**." Start your adventure with Marina Beach, one of the world's longest urban beaches, where visitors and residents alike congregate to take in the breathtaking sunsets and sea air. Famous sites like the Senate House and the Triumph of Labour monument border the Marina, creating a lovely setting for this vibrant area.

Exploring the history of the city's colonial past is possible with a visit to Fort St. George, the first English garrison in India. Within its walls, the Fort Museum displays British-era relics that provide light on Chennai's historical development. Take a stroll around George Town, the former business district, to see the opulence of buildings such as the High Court and the Parry's Corner skyscraper.

Visit the amazing Kapaleeshwarar Temple in Mylapore, a temple devoted to Lord Shiva and a wonder of Dravidian architecture, to get a glimpse of the city's spiritual side. With its busy Mylapore neighborhood and its tiny lanes filled with brightly colored buildings, street sellers, and the delicious smells of regional food, the area is a microcosm of traditional Tamil life.

Historical Landmarks

Chennai is home to a multitude of historical sites that tell the tale of the city's development. The second-oldest museum in India, the Government Museum was founded in 1851 and has a vast collection of artifacts, numismatics, and archeological discoveries among other items. The museum's Bronze Gallery is especially notable for its magnificent collection of prehistoric bronze sculptures from South India.

One of the main pilgrimage sites, San Thome Basilica, is located on the grave of St. Thomas, one of the twelve apostles of Jesus Christ. It offers a peaceful haven from the bustle of the city thanks to its neo-Gothic architecture and quiet atmosphere.

An insight into Chennai's administrative past may be gained by seeing the renowned Ripon Building, an architectural marvel constructed in the Indo-Saracenic style. The Greater Chennai Corporation is housed in a structure with elaborate carvings and stained glass windows.

Cultural Hotspots

With so many theaters, music academies, and art galleries, Chennai is a city brimming with cultural activity. Kalakshetra is a place where ancient Indian arts are preserved. It hosts dance and music events in beautiful gardens. Situated a short drive from the city, the DakshinaChitra Museum has handicrafts, relics, and reconstructed traditional dwellings that highlight the many cultures of South India.

For lovers of classical music, the city becomes a paradise of Carnatic music performances during the Margazhi season, which takes place in December and January. Renowned locations such as the Music Academy and Narada Gana Sabha are used by master performers and up-and-coming performers to captivate audiences with emotionally charged shows.

The Cholamandal Artists' Village, a community of artists with a gallery showcasing modern and traditional Indian art, is a must-see for art enthusiasts. The village is evidence of Chennai's contribution to the development of contemporary Indian art.

Shopping and Dining

For those who are excited to discover the city's culinary and shopping gems, Chennai's markets and restaurants provide a fascinating adventure. Start your shopping adventure at T. Nagar, a busy business area renowned for its vivacious street markets and posh stores. The primary retail district in the neighborhood, Pondy Bazaar, is a bustling place to buy jewelry, traditional handicrafts, and silk sarees.

Visit the famed Chennai Silks store, known for its magnificent silk sarees, in the ancient GeorgeTown district for a unique shopping experience. The packed alleys of Parry's Corner are a treasure trove for those looking for unusual objects, spices, and textiles.

Chennai's food scene is a delicious blend of international influences and traditional South Indian cuisines. Start your culinary adventure with the highly regarded worldwide brand Saravana Bhavan, which offers real vegetarian South Indian food. Royapuram's streets are filled with alternatives for seafood lovers, ranging from expensive seafood restaurants to modest roadside shops.

Savor the city's well-known filter coffee at one of the many cafés in Mylapore; the fragrant brew is proof of Chennai's passion for this drink. Dakshin at the Crowne Plaza provides a well-prepared cuisine highlighting the many South Indian culinary traditions for a wonderful dining experience.

To sum up, Chennai, a thriving city at the nexus of modernity and tradition, extends a warm welcome to everyone who arrives. Chennai provides the ideal environment for an enthralling introduction to Tamil Nadu's treasures, with its historical sites, cultural hotspots, and varied cuisine. It also offers shopping opportunities for traditional goods.

SOUTHERN SPLENDORS - Madurai and Rameswaram

Set off on an adventure through the breathtaking southern cities of Madurai and Rameswaram, where Tamil Nadu's spiritual zeal and cultural diversity come to life. Both pilgrims and visitors are enthralled with the tapestry of experiences that these two historically significant locations have to offer.

Madurai, The City of Temples:

Known as the "**Athens of the East**," Madurai is a symbol of Tamil Nadu's rich cultural history. The Meenakshi Amman Temple, a wonder of Dravidian architecture, is located in the center of it. The temple complex, dedicated to Goddess Meenakshi and Lord Sundareswarar, is a maze of elaborately carved mandapams **(halls)**, shrines, and gopurams. The epic stories of Hindu mythology are told in the Hall of Thousand Pillars, which is ornamented with finely carved pillars.

A feast for the senses may be found in the Meenakshi Bazaar, the busy lanes that encircle the temple. Brightly colored booths display jewelry with exquisite designs, silk sarees, and traditional items. The market's vivid colors and the air filled with the scent of jasmine blossoms both capture the vitality of Madurai's cultural culture.

Explore the Thirumalai Nayak Palace, a blend of Islamic and Dravidian architectural traditions, located beyond the Meenakshi Amman Temple. The magnificent Swarga Vilasam Hall, the courtyard, and the imposing pillars all showcase the palace's magnificence. See the enchanted Meenakshi Thirukalyanam in the evening, a traditional bridal procession that draws both visitors and believers.

Rameswaram,Retreat to the Island:
Situated on Pamban Island, Rameswaram is both a serene island getaway and a hallowed place of worship. One of the twelve Jyotirlinga temples devoted to Lord Shiva, the Ramanathaswamy Temple, is the town's most famous landmark. To conduct the auspicious Sethu Pooja, which entails worshiping Lord Rama and asking for blessings at the sacred location where, according to legend, Lord Rama constructed a bridge to Lanka, pilgrims go to Rameswaram.

The Ramanathaswamy Temple is an architectural wonder, with its lengthy hallways and enormous carved pillars. The holy sea bathing place Agnitheertham enhances the meditative atmosphere. In addition to being an architectural wonder in and of itself, the Pamban Bridge, which links Rameswaram to the Indian mainland, provides stunning views of the surrounding waterways.

Travelers are drawn to Rameswaram's tranquil beaches, which lie beyond the holy sites. Tales of a bygone period may be found in Dhanushkodi, a ghost town located near the southeast extremity of the island. A feeling of peace and seclusion is produced by the ethereal landscapes, which include the Indian Ocean and the Bay of Bengal on opposite sides.

Pilgrimage Routes and Rituals

Traveling to Madurai and Rameswaram is a pilgrimage through Tamil Nadu's spiritual center as well as a physical discovery. Following in the footsteps of saints and sages, pilgrims often travel the spiritual circuit, linking these two towns with other hallowed locations.

Join the pilgrimage known as the Pancha Sabhai Kshetrams in Madurai. This pilgrimage takes you to five halls of worship where Lord Shiva is said to have performed cosmic dances. The voyage is an absorption into the holy spirit that pervades these hallowed sites, not simply about being physically there.

The spiritual pilgrimage at Rameswaram continues to the Agni Teertham, where followers bathe ceremoniously before entering the Ramanathaswamy Temple. A key component of the pilgrimage experience is participating in temple rituals, such as giving prayers and seeing the god. Seeking blessings and cleansing, pilgrims often circle the island to end their spiritual journey.

Local Food and Markets

Madurai and Rameswaram's delectable cuisines provide a scrumptious introduction to Tamil Nadu's traditional flavors. With its spicy food, Madurai offers a wide variety of gastronomic delights. At the well-known Murugan Idli Shop, begin your day with a typical South Indian breakfast. Savor steaming idlis and crispy dosas accompanied by a variety of chutneys and sambar.

Go into the busy streets around the Meenakshi Amman Temple to get a sample of the street cuisine there. Sample the well-known Jigarthanda, a refreshing beverage prepared with milk, ice cream, sarsaparilla root syrup, and almond gum that is a great way to escape the heat of the city.

Because Rameswaram is located near the seaside, seafood is the main attraction there. A wide range of fresh catches, including fish and crabs as well as prawns, are available at the neighborhood markets. Visit the Shri Meenakshi Cold Storage to buy seafood and take in the lively vibe of the marketplace.

Look for trinkets and regional handicrafts at Rameswaram's marketplaces. The village is well-known for its elaborately carved, lucky conch shell items. A wonderful fusion of culture and artistry can be seen in the local markets, which also sell elaborate idols, jewelry made of seashells, and traditional handwoven silk sarees.

In summary, the spirituality, history, and cultural richness of the southern wonders of Madurai and Rameswaram are intricately woven together. This tour into the heart of Tamil Nadu offers an immersive experience that remains in the spirit, from the spectacular temples and ceremonies that resound with centuries-old traditions to the calm beaches and tasty food.

TRANQUIL COASTS - Coastal Towns and Beaches:

Over a thousand kilometers of gorgeous coastal towns and immaculate beaches border Tamil Nadu's coastline along the Bay of Bengal, beckoning visitors to enjoy the tranquil beauty of the ocean. The coastal area of Tamil Nadu provides a variety of experiences, from the ancient Tranquebar with its Danish connection to the sculptural wonders of Mahabalipuram and the peaceful beach getaways.

Tranquebar, Danish connection:

The intriguing Danish ancestry of Tranquebar, often referred to as Tharangambadi, gives it a special position in Tamil Nadu's coastal environment. This charming hamlet, which is tucked away along the Coromandel Coast, was formerly a Danish trade port in the seventeenth century. The remnants of this history can still be seen in the town's colonial architecture.

The famous Fort Dansborg, which the Danes erected at the beginning of the 17th century, is proof of Tranquebar's historical importance. The fort provides expansive views of the sea from its watchtowers and strong walls. Another architectural treasure that exhibits the Danish influence is the 1701-er Zion Church, which has a calm atmosphere and a Baroque-style building.

The peaceful beaches of Tranquebar are ideal for strolling along, while the colonial buildings and Danish Fort provide a striking background. The town's marine museum, which displays Danish-era relics, deepens the historical investigation. The combination of history, the sea, and culture in Tranquebar creates an enchanted place that takes visitors back in time.

Mahabalipuram, Sculptures by the Sea:
Mahabalipuram, a seaside resort renowned for its magnificent stone sculptures and temples, is also known for its UNESCO World Heritage-listed Group of Monuments. These monuments, which were carved in the 7th and 8th centuries under the Pallava dynasty, are evidence of the artistic and architectural excellence of prehistoric Tamil culture.

Perched on the Bay of Bengal, the Shore Temple is a wonder of Dravidian architecture. At dawn and dusk, the temple radiates a mysterious atmosphere as the sea's waves caress its old stones. There are five chariot-shaped temples in the Pancha Rathas, a collection of monolithic rock-cut temples, each honoring a different deity. Two enormous stones have been carved with a large bas-relief called Arjuna's Penance, which depicts episodes from Hindu mythology.

The town's well-known Descent of the Ganges monument, often called Arjuna's Penance, is a huge outdoor sculpture that tells a Mahabharata tale. For those who are interested in history and art, the site is appealing because of its delicate workmanship and elaborate carvings.

Not only is Mahabalipuram a historical gem, but its sandy beaches provide a tranquil haven. Resorts and cafés dot the shoreline, offering the ideal combination of leisure and cultural discovery. The colorful Mamallapuram Dance Festival, which takes place in front of the monuments, draws classical dancers from all over the nation, giving the historic town a modern cultural edge.

Beach Escapes and Water Activities:

The coastal area of Tamil Nadu is home to a multitude of beach getaways, each providing a distinctive combination of peace and excitement. One of the longest urban beaches in the world, Marina Beach in Chennai is a busy stretch where visitors and residents congregate for promenade strolls, horseback rides, and street food vendors.

A little farther down the coast, Kanyakumari's calm beaches provide a peaceful haven. A distinctive seascape is produced by the Arabian Sea, Bay of Bengal, and Indian Ocean coming together. From the southernmost point of India, where the Vivekananda Rock Memorial and the Thiruvalluvar Statue watch silently over the land, take in the spectacular sunrises and sunsets.

Tamil Nadu's coastal towns provide fascinating activities for water lovers. In locations like Covelong and Mahabalipuram, surfing and windsurfing courses draw both novice and expert surfers. The Bay of Bengal's mild waves provide it the perfect backdrop for water sports, and the region's instructors guarantee a fun and safe experience.

Divers who like scuba diving may discover the underwater treasures off the coast of Puducherry, home to a variety of marine life and colorful coral reefs. For diving excursions, the Bay of Bengal's pristine waters provide exceptional visibility.

In conclusion, visitors are invited to discover a rich tapestry of history, culture, and natural beauty along Tamil Nadu's serene coastlines. A must-visit location for anyone looking for a seaside getaway with cultural depth, the coastal area provides a beautiful combination of leisure and discovery, from the historical ties of Tranquebar to the sculptural marvels of Mahabalipuram and the varied beach retreats.

TEMPLE TRAILS - Thanjavur and Trichy

Traveling the Thanjavur and Trichy temple paths is a voyage into the center of Tamil Nadu's cultural and religious legacy. These temple-studded towns tell stories of empires, beautiful art, and the centuries-long spiritual passion that has shaped the area.

Thanjavur-Art and Architectures:

Often referred to as the "Cultural Capital of the State" and the "Rice Bowl of Tamil Nadu," Thanjavur is a witness to the magnificence of Chola architecture as well as the creative talent of Tamil craftsmen. The centerpiece of Thanjavur's temple landscape is the Brihadeeswarar Temple, often referred to as the Big Temple. It is a UNESCO World Heritage site. Constructed in the eleventh century by Rajaraja Chola I, this enormous temple to Lord Shiva is a masterpiece of architecture.

Reaching an astounding height, the majestic vimana **(temple tower)** is crowned with a gigantic granite dome. The temple displays the skill of Chola artists with its elaborate sculptures and well-painted murals that narrate themes from Hindu mythology. The entrance is guarded by the nearly 25-ton monolithic sculpture known as the Nandi Bull, which further contributes to the temple's imposing atmosphere.

The Thanjavur Palace, an architectural marvel that housed the Nayak and Maratha monarchs, is located next to the Brihadeeswarar Temple. The Saraswathi Mahal Library, housed in the royal complex, is renowned for its rare volumes and collection of old palm-leaf manuscripts.

The vivid Tanjore paintings, which date back to the 16th century and were created at the Thanjavur Maratha court, are another reason for Thanjavur's fame. These paintings, which are valued as cultural treasures and often include mythical subjects, are distinguished by their rich, brilliant colors and elaborate gold leaf work.

Trich-Religious Heritage and Rock Fort:
Trichy, also known as Tiruchirapalli, is a city that skillfully combines modernity with tradition. The famous Rock Fort, a huge rock structure with panoramic city views and ancient temples inside, is the center of the city. Lord Ganesha is worshiped in the rock-top Ucchi Pillayar Temple. In addition to providing a spiritual experience, ascending the

temple's 434 steps rewards climbers with breathtaking views of the surroundings.

The Lord Shiva-focused Thayumanavar Temple is located at the foot of the Rock Fort. The elaborate sculptures and colorful surrounds of the temple heighten the atmosphere of spirituality. A massive temple pond nearby called Teppakulam Pond is encircled by mandapams or pavilions. It is the venue of the Float Festival, a major event in which deities are paraded on floating platforms.

Another stunning example of Trichy architecture is the Sri Ranganathaswamy Temple, which is perched on an island in the Kaveri River. Lord Ranganatha, a reclining version of Lord Vishnu, is the object of devotion at this, one of the biggest Hindu temples still in operation worldwide. The temple is a must-see for both believers and architectural aficionados because of its magnificent gopurams, elaborate sculptures, and the Hall of Thousand Pillars.

Situated near Trichy, on the Srirangam island, the Jambukeswarar Temple is one of the Pancha Bhoota Stalas, symbolizing the element of water. A lingam immersed in water is kept in the temple's sanctuary, signifying the holy bond between Lord Shiva and the element of water.

Festivals and Celebrations:

During festivals and celebrations, the temple paths in Thanjavur and Trichy spring to life, offering a comprehensive look into Tamil Nadu's vibrant religious and cultural life. The Brihadeeswarar Temple's Arudra Darshanam festival, held in Thanjavur, is a noteworthy occasion when the deity is decorated with unique rites and processions. Every year, during Mahashivaratri, there is an annual Natyanjali Dance Festival that draws classical dancers from all around the nation who perform acts of devotion.

The Teppakulam Tank Float Festival in Trichy is a magnificent occasion when gods are carried in a parade on the tank while adorned with exquisite floats. Witnessing the spectacle of the ceremony, which is a visual feast of colors and religious zeal, devotees and onlookers assemble.

The Sri Ranganathaswamy Temple at Srirangam, a suburb of Trichy, is the site of the Vaikunta Ekadasi festival. The Vaikunta Dwaram is a unique entryway that is only accessible on this day, and devotees think that entering it leads to salvation. The lights and decorations within the temple create a heavenly ambiance.

Homes and temples around Thanjavur and Trichy light oil lamps as part of the Karthigai Deepam festival, which is a festival of lights. The whole area is lit up, resulting in a mystical atmosphere that represents the victory of light over darkness.

To sum up, the temple trails in Thanjavur and Trichy provide an exploration of Tamil Nadu's essence, a place where spirituality, art, and architecture come together. These towns serve as enduring reminders of the rich customs that have defined the area for millennia, from the magnificence of the Brihadeeswarar Temple to the rock-cut temples of Trichy and the colorful festivals that honor the cultural legacy.

HILL STATIONS - Ooty and Kodaikanal

Explore the captivating allure of the Western Ghats by traveling to the hill towns of Kodaikanal and Ooty. These locations, which are tucked away among tranquil lakes, verdant tea gardens, and mist-covered mountains, provide the ideal getaway from the stress of daily life. Discover the Princess of Hill Stations, Kodaikanal, and the Queen of the Nilgiris, Ooty, as they reveal a tapestry of breathtaking sights and enjoyable activities.

Ooty: Queen of the Nilgiris

Ooty, sometimes referred to as Udhagamandalam, is the Nilgiri Hills' crown gem. Situated at 2,240 meters above sea level, this hill station has been dubbed the "**Queen of the Nilgiris**" because of its amazing scenery, comfortable weather, and classic Victorian ambiance. The drive to Ooty is just as charming as the place itself, with its meandering roads providing sweeping vistas of misted mountains and tea plantations.

A UNESCO World Heritage site, the Nilgiri Mountain Railway transports visitors on a nostalgic ride through twists and turns and verdant scenery. The toy train journey from

Mettupalayam to Ooty is a fascinating experience that gives you a peek at the stunning scenery of the Nilgiri Hills.

The Ooty Lake, a picturesque body of water bordered by eucalyptus trees and providing boat excursions with expansive vistas, is the focal point of Ooty. Founded in 1847, the Botanical Gardens have an extensive variety of exotic trees, flowers, and plants. Nature lovers will find visual enjoyment in the rose garden, which is home to hundreds of species of roses.

The Nilgiris' highest peak, Doddabetta Peak, provides stunning vistas of the lowlands and hillsides below. With its vivid hues and aromatic blossoms, the 4-hectare Government Rose Garden is a haven for rose enthusiasts. The town's old-world appeal is enhanced by the lovely colonial architecture of St. Stephen's Church and the Ooty Railway Station.

Kodaikanal: The Princess of Hill Stations

Boasted in the Western Ghats' Palani Hills, Kodaikanal lives up to its title as the "Princess of Hill Stations" thanks to its foggy vistas, forested hillsides, and immaculate lakes. Traveling to Kodaikanal offers a breathtaking view of verdant trees and winding roads that lead to this peaceful haven.

The town's focal point is Kodaikanal Lake, an artificial lake with a star form. The tranquility of the lake surrounded by hills covered with trees may be experienced by guests using pedal boats and rowing boats. Bryant Park, along the lake, has rafts of water lilies and a varied assortment of flowers and hybrids.

A beautiful promenade called Coaker's Walk provides amazing views of the plains, valleys, and hills in the area. Three enormous granite boulders known as the Pillar Rocks are seen against a background of mist-covered mountains. Suicide Point, sometimes called Green Valley View, offers expansive views of the deep valleys and plains.

For those who like the outdoors, Berijam Lake is a tranquil location surrounded by thick trees. Reachable by special authorization from the Forest Service, the lake provides a tranquil haven from the busy town. Amidst the verdant surroundings, the 180-foot-tall Silver Cascade Waterfall on the Ghat Road creates a charming backdrop.

Nature Walks and Adventure Activities:

Ooty and Kodaikanal provide plenty of chances for nature lovers and adventure seekers to enjoy their immaculate landscapes. Surrounded by verdant tea plantations, Ooty offers a glimpse of the tea-making process with a visit to one of the estates. Trekking and nature hikes are welcome in the Nilgiri Biosphere Reserve, which is home to a wide variety of plants and animals. The Bengal tiger and Nilgiri tahr inhabit the Mukurthi National Park, which is a component of the biosphere reserve and a wildlife enthusiast's paradise.

Trekking routes in Kodaikanal lead to captivating vistas and undiscovered treasures. Views of the Western Ghats may be seen in all directions from The Dolphin's Nose, a flat rock that protrudes over a magnificent abyss. Adventurers who climb the tallest mountain in the area, Perumal Mountain, are rewarded with breathtaking views and a feeling of achievement.

The Ooty Botanical Gardens in Ooty and Coaker's Walk in Kodaikanal provide peaceful settings for strolls for people looking for a peaceful experience. Both sites highlight the region's varied vegetation, which includes colorful flowers, fragrant herbs, and old trees.

Both hill villages provide adventure sports like rock climbing and paragliding, which provide visitors with a burst of excitement among the tranquil scenery. The pristine sky and undulating hills of Ooty provide the perfect backdrop for thrilling paragliding experiences. Because of Kodaikanal's rough terrain, adventure seekers may enjoy the natural splendor while engaging in exhilarating sports like rock climbing and rappelling.

To sum up, visitors are drawn to the hill stations of Ooty and Kodaikanal by their breathtaking scenery, comfortable weather, and plenty of activities. These locations, with their colonial charm in Ooty and their foggy vistas in Kodaikanal, provide the ideal fusion of adventure, nature, and peace, making them classic getaways for anybody looking for a change of pace from everyday life.

WILDLIFE ADVENTURES - Periyar National Park

Tucked away in Kerala's Western Ghats, Periyar National Park—officially named Periyar Tiger Reserve—serves as a haven for aficionados of wildlife and the natural world. This verdant stretch of protected territory is a sanctuary for a wide variety of plants and animals, offering a riveting combination of breathtaking scenery and exhilarating wildlife encounters. Let's discover Periyar's distinct appeal by venturing into its forest.

Exploring Periyar Tiger Reserve:
The 925-square-kilometer Periyar Tiger Reserve is a symbol of the area's dedication to the preservation of wildlife. The stunning Periyar Lake, an artificial reservoir made possible by the Mullaperiyar Dam, is the focal point of the reserve. This large body of water not only provides vital water for the species but also adds to the reserve's picturesque appeal.

The possibility of boat safaris is one of Periyar's special attractions. Witnessing animals in their natural home is made both peacefully and excitingly possible with Periyar Lake boat trips. A symphony of noises, from the cry of exotic birds to the rustling of leaves signaling the movement of invisible animals, is accompanied by the lush shoreline. Elephants often approach the water's edge for a cool swim, giving tourists unforgettable sights.

Periyar provides guided nature hikes and hiking options in addition to boat safaris. These excursions take guests far into the forest, allowing them to discover the many ecosystems and get up close and personal with some of the more elusive species. Every stride through Periyar is a journey into the unknown due to its vast biodiversity and diverse landscapes, which encourage a spirit of adventure and discovery.

Flora and Fauna:
With its meadows, water basins, and tropical evergreen and deciduous woods, Periyar National Park is a veritable gold mine of biodiversity. The park's diverse altitudes support a large variety of plant life by serving as homes for a broad spectrum of plant species.

A wide range of tree species, including teak, rosewood, sandalwood, and bamboo, may be found in the wet deciduous woods. With their thick canopy, the evergreen woods are home to a wide variety of flora, including mosses and orchids that like the moist environment as well as enormous trees.

Periyar is a wildlife enthusiast's dream come true because of its similarly diversified fauna. Indian elephants are the park's most famous inhabitants, and boat safaris on Periyar Lake often provide up-close looks at these magnificent animals when they come to drink.

The park is also home to the elusive and endangered Bengal tiger, however, sightings are uncommon because of the thick undergrowth. Mammals that live in Periyar include leopards, Indian bison **(gaur)**, sambar deer, barking deer, and wild boars. The Nilgiri langur, lion-tailed macaque, and Malabar giant squirrel inhabit the park, which lends elegance to the canopy.

Birdwatchers will enjoy Periyar's wide variety of birds. There are now around 260 species of birds known to exist, such as the colorful Malabar trogon, Nilgiri wood pigeon, and Malabar grey hornbill. The park's sources of water attract a wide diversity of water birds, which enhances the sight of birds.

Safari Experiences:

To discover its varied landscapes and get up close with its local animals, Periyar provides a variety of safari opportunities. Witnessing animals gathered at the water's edge is a serene but thrilling experience offered by the boat safari on Periyar Lake. The serene lake's surface, reflecting the verdant surroundings, heightens the enchanted atmosphere.

Jeep safaris allow the discovery of a variety of habitats and topography by taking guests deeper into the reserve's primary sections. Accompanying the safaris are knowledgeable guides who provide information about the park's vegetation, animals, and conservation initiatives. When it comes to seeing bigger species and visiting places that are not accessible by water, vehicle safaris are particularly beneficial.

Trekking routes and guided nature hikes are available in Periyar for those looking for a more immersive experience. Through the routes through the forest, these trips provide guests with a close-up view of the natural world. For those who join these nature walks, the sounds of the forest, the rustling of leaves, and the potential to see animals up close make for an unforgettable experience.

Bamboo rafting is another unusual pastime available in Periyar. Participants in this environmentally friendly excursion navigate Periyar Lake's lush trees while riding a bamboo raft. Sliding softly through the water, people may watch animals from a new angle and feel a stronger connection to the natural world.

Periyar Tiger Reserve actively participates in community-based ecotourism projects and animal protection in addition to offering safari experiences. The park has put in place several initiatives to include neighborhood residents in conservation efforts, striking a healthy balance between the preservation of wildlife and environmentally friendly travel.

In summary, Periyar National Park provides a haven for a wide variety of plants and animals, serving as a monument to the natural beauties of the Western Ghats. Every time spent in Periyar is a chance to engage with nature, whether you want to go on a guided nature walk, take a jeep safari into the heart of the forest, or explore the serene waters of Periyar Lake on a boat safari.

CULTURAL EXPERIENCES - Music, Dance, and Arts:

Traveling through a region's cultural tapestry is like walking onto a colorful painting where attitudes, customs, and aesthetic subtleties all come together to tell a tale of identity and legacy. Tamil Nadu's traditional music, dances, handicrafts, and festivals all reflect the profound integration of cultural events into day-to-day living. Let's investigate the diverse cultural landscape that makes Tamil Nadu a veritable gold mine of creative expression.

Traditional Dance and Music:
Called the "**Land of Tamils**," Tamil Nadu has a rich history of traditional arts that have thrived for centuries.

Carnatic music is a traditional style that has developed over millennia and is the foundation of Tamil Nadu's musical heritage. Carnatic music, which is recognized for its complex rhythms and melodic scales, is a spiritual journey conveyed by vocalists and musicians using instruments like the veena, violin, and mridangam. Chennai's Margazhi season, which is celebrated with concerts and music festivals, draws artists and fans from all over the globe.

Bharatanatyam: The expressive gestures and rhythmic footwork of this traditional dance style are hallmarks of visual poetry that reveals stories from Hindu mythology. The dance combines raga **(melody)**, tala **(rhythm)**, and natya **(expression)** beautifully. Events are sometimes held in ornately decorated temples or other cultural venues, where performers captivate spectators with the delicacy and dexterity of every gesture.

Folk Music and Dance: The rich cultural variety of Tamil Nadu is reflected in the lively folk music and dance styles that flourish outside of the classical sphere. Oyilattam, a rhythmic dance to traditional music, and karakattam, a folk dance in which artists balance pots on their heads, both highlight the happiness and celebrations inherent in the local communities.

Crafts and Art:

Tamil Nadu's arts and crafts are evidence of the skill and creative grace that have been handed down through the years.

Tanjore painting is a classic style of South Indian painting that is distinguished by its images of deities, gold leaf decorations, and rich, vibrant colors. The village of Thanjavur gave rise to this renowned art style, which is being practiced today. Artists painstakingly create works of mythology and religion.

Chola Bronze Sculptures: Beautiful bronze sculptures are a lasting testament to the creative heritage of the Chola empire. These sculptures, which are made of lost wax casting, show gods, goddesses, and other celestial creatures. These classic pieces are brought to life by talented craftspeople at the bronze studios located in Swamimalai, Kumbakonam, and other cities.

Kanjivaram Silk Sarees: Known for its vivid hues and dexterous zari embroidery, the Kanjivaram silk saree epitomizes South Indian grace. These traditional-patterned sarees, woven in the town of Kanchipuram, are a staple of wedding trousseau and celebratory wear.

Papier Mâché Dolls: The town of Tirupattur is home to a thriving papier mâché doll-making industry. Paper pulp is molded by artisans into exquisite dolls that represent a variety of folkloric, mythological, and everyday figures. The dolls are often painted in vivid colors, which lends a touch of creativity to residences and cultural gatherings.

Local Cultural Events & Festivals:
Tamil Nadu is a region of festivals, each one a magnificent display of ancient customs and cultural enthusiasm.

Pongal: The harvest festival, Pongal, is an occasion to express thankfulness to the natural world. Brightly colored rice flour kolams, or rangoli, decorate homes, and traditional meals like Pongal—a dish made with freshly harvested rice—are cooked. The festival often features Jallikattu, or bull-taming activities, which highlight the bravery and tenacity of rural people.

Madurai Chithirai Festival: This great event, which recreates the heavenly marriage of Lord Meenakshi and Lord Sundareswarar, brings the city to life. Over many weeks, there are processions, cultural shows, and the magnificent Chariot Festival, which includes the parade of gods through the streets.

The Natyanjali Dance Festival is a gathering of classical dancers who present their dance performances as a form of adoration to Lord Shiva. It takes place in the historic

Chidambaram Nataraja Temple. The event turns the hallowed area into a visual and spiritual extravaganza against the background of the temple's stunning architecture.

Karthigai Deepam: Tamil Nadu celebrates the festival of lights, Karthigai Deepam, with great enthusiasm. Temples are ornamented with many lights, while homes are lit with oil lamps. The beautiful ritual of lighting the massive flame atop Thiruvannamalai Hill attracts both pilgrims and visitors.

Tamil Nadu's cultural experiences are not limited to certain occasions; rather, they are a part of daily existence. The fragrances of traditional food, temple rites, and street entertainment all add to the full cultural environment. Because of the state's dedication to protecting and promoting its cultural legacy, every visit becomes a trip through time where antiquated customs coexist peacefully with modern manifestations.

EXPLORING TAMIL NADU ON A BUDGET: Unveiling Affordable Delights

Even travelers on a tight budget may enjoy a variety of activities in Tamil Nadu, a state rich in history and culture. This South Indian state offers a wealth of affordable activities, including historic temples and gorgeous scenery. Together, we will explore Tamil Nadu on a budget, enjoying reasonably priced local food, lodging that fits our needs, and free or inexpensive attractions.

Free and low-cost attractions:

The Shore Temple at Mahabalipuram and Arjuna's Penance: Mahabalipuram, a UNESCO World Heritage site, greets guests with free architectural marvels. Admiring the Bay of Bengal, the Shore Temple is an exquisite example of Dravidian architecture. Next to it is Arjuna's Penance, a massive relief sculpture of Hindu mythological images on two monolithic rocks. Discovering these historic treasures is a free way to get a taste of the rich history of the area.

Marina Beach, Chennai: One of the world's longest urban beaches, Marina Beach welcomes guests to relax on its sandy shores at no cost. Enjoy the saline wind, take a leisurely walk, and take in the colorful local culture. There are expansive views of the coastline from the famous lighthouse next to the beach.

Rock Fort, Trichy: Combining religious importance with stunning vistas, the Rock Fort in Trichy is a historic landmark. A modest admission charge allows you to see the city's expansive panorama and centuries-old architecture at the ancient temples situated atop the rock-cut stairs.

Kanyakumari Dawn and Sunset: Kanyakumari, the southernmost part of India, provides breathtaking views of the dawn and sunset, and it is completely free to take in these natural marvels. The experience is enhanced by the confluence of the Indian Ocean, Bay of Bengal, and Arabian Sea. Other sites to consider include the Vivekananda Rock Memorial and Thiruvalluvar Statue, although with a small admission price.

Affordable Eateries:

Saravana Bhavan: Known for its tasty and reasonably priced South Indian vegetarian food, Saravana Bhavan has locations all across Tamil Nadu and even beyond. With options ranging from crunchy dosas to delectable curries, the large menu pleases a wide range of pallets without breaking the bank.

Madurai is renowned for its excellent and reasonably priced street cuisine. Wander around the busy streets around Meenakshi Amman Temple, where you can get a range of foods including spicy chaats, jigar thanda (a local beverage), and kothu parotta. Snacking on these tasty treats won't break the bank.

Murugan Idli Shop: This inexpensive find is well-known for having some of Tamil Nadu's fluffiest idlis. Situated in many towns, this restaurant is popular among both residents and tourists because of its delicious but straightforward cuisine.

Karaikudi, located in the Chettinad district, is well-known for its distinctive and fiery Chettinad food. Visit neighborhood restaurants to enjoy reasonably priced dishes such as kara kuzhambu, Chettinad chicken curry, and a selection of dosas.

Budget-Friendly Accommodations:
Hostels & Guesthouses: Tamil Nadu offers a variety of reasonably priced hostels and guesthouses to suit the

demands of tourists on a tight budget. You may find reasonably priced, cozy lodging with shared amenities in places like Pondicherry, Madurai, and Chennai.

Chettinad Heritage Homestays: The area provides a unique chance to stay in historical buildings that have been turned into guesthouses. Discover the region's rich cultural legacy while staying in reasonably priced lodging in charming settings.

Government Guest Homes: The government runs guest homes in several Tamil Nadu cities, providing reasonably priced lodging. These guest rooms are an affordable choice for tourists as they often provide basic facilities and are kept up properly.

Ooty and Kodaikanal Budget Hotels: Well-known hill towns like Ooty and Kodaikanal provide reasonably priced lodging options that offer cozy stays without breaking the bank. These hotels often have lovely views of the surroundings.

With a wide range of attractions and a vibrant culture, Tamil Nadu welcomes visitors on a budget. Discovering historic temples, sampling regional food, or sleeping in reasonably priced lodgings—the state's allure is still within reach for those on a tight budget. Accept Tamil Nadu's splendor without going over budget, and allow the adventures to happen at a speed that works for your heart and your pocketbook.

CULINARY DELIGHTS OF TAMIL NADU: A Gastronomic Journey Through South Indian Flavors

In addition to its colorful customs and old temples, Tamil Nadu, a cultural and historical treasure in South India, is well-known for its extensive and varied culinary legacy. Deeply ingrained in history and taste, the state's cuisine presents a delightful tapestry of South Indian delicacies. Tamil Nadu's culinary marvels entice food connoisseurs on a trip that tantalizes the taste senses with its distinct blend of spices and cooking methods. Let's explore the culinary delights of this area, including South Indian specialties, meals you really must taste, and the exciting world of street food and neighborhood restaurants.

Food from South India:
South Indian food, which is mostly contributed by Tamil Nadu, is known for its concentration of rice, lentils, coconut, and a variety of spices that come together to produce a harmonious blend of tastes.

Idli and dosa: It would be incomplete to discuss South Indian food without bringing up idli and dosa. Breakfast staples include dosas, which are thin rice crepes, and idlis, which are steamed rice cakes. Accompanied by tart sambar, a lentil-based vegetable stew, and coconut chutney, these dishes highlight the region's fondness for fermented rice and urad dal (**black gram**).

Sambhar and Rasam: A staple side dish in South Indian cuisine, sambhar is a spiced, lentil-based vegetable stew with tamarind. Colds may be cured and comfort food enjoyed in equal measure with raita, a spicy, sour soup prepared with tamarind and tomatoes. These tasty mixtures may be eaten as stand-alone soups or with rice.

Chettinad Cuisine: This cuisine, which originated in the Chettinad area, is well-known for its robust tastes and liberal use of spices. Must-try dishes include the aromatic rice dish Chettinad biryani and the chicken curry created with a special combination of spices. A delicious take on the original, the masala dosa is the region's hallmark dish, including a spicy potato filling.

Coffee Filter: A staple of South Indian culture, filter coffee is a ceremonial aspect of everyday life in Tamil Nadu. The robust and fragrant coffee is prepared by pouring boiling water through ground coffee beans in a metal filter and serving it in a dabara **(cup)** and stainless steel tumbler. It is often served with a portion of foamy milk that has been sweetened to taste.

Recipes You Must Try:
Many dishes in Tamil Nadu's cuisine showcase the region's variety and intricate culinary techniques.

Chennai Biryani: A tribute to the city's culinary skill, Chennai biryani is a fragrant and savory rice dish. A symphony of tastes is created when basmati rice is cooked with fragrant spices, soft meat **(often chicken or mutton)**, and an unidentified masala mix. It's usually served with a refreshing raita.

Meen Kuzhambu (Fish Curry): Tamil Nadu's long coastline makes it a seafood lover's paradise. A zesty and hot fish curry, Meen Kuzhambu is a culinary masterpiece. A thick and fragrant sauce that accentuates the freshness of the fish is made with tamarind, coconut, and a variety of spices.

Pongal: Enjoying a meal of the same name is a must-do while celebrating the harvest festival. Traditionally, ghee, cumin, and pepper are used to season pongal, a savory porridge made with rice and lentils. As a sign of prosperity, it is often consumed during the celebration with a side of coconut chutney.

Atho-Burmese Delight in Chennai: Atho, a Burmese-inspired noodle salad, is the latest offering from Chennai's bustling street food scene. Atho, which is inspired by the cosmopolitan vibe of the city, consists of flat noodles combined with a range of raw and cooked ingredients, such as cabbage, egg, and a unique hot sauce.

Local Restaurants and Street Food:
The streets of Tamil Nadu are a colorful culinary canvas, with a wide variety of tastes available from neighborhood restaurants and street food sellers.

Kothu Parotta: This delicious street food delicacy is exclusive to Madurai. Layers of soft, stacked flatbreads called parottas are stir-fried with a mixture of veggies, eggs, and seasonings after being shredded. It is popular among both residents and tourists because of its alluring scent and distinctive texture.

Jigarthanda: A refreshing drink indigenous to Madurai, Jigarthanda will quench your thirst. A wonderful drink that is a must-try for anybody visiting Madurai's busy streets, this mixture of almond gum, sarsaparilla root syrup, milk, and ice cream offers a sweet relief from the heat.

Marina Beach's Sundal: Marina Beach, one of the world's longest urban beaches, has more to offer than simply beautiful scenery. Sundal, a tasty and high-protein snack prepared from boiling legumes like chickpeas or black-eyed peas, is sold by a plethora of sellers along the coast. Sunday, a tasty snack loved by beachgoers, is seasoned with mustard seeds, curry leaves, and shredded coconut.

Kanyakumari's "**small samosa**," or Chinna Samosa, is a treat for foodies. The town is well-known for its breathtaking sunsets. These little samosas, filled with spicy potatoes or veggies, are the ideal light meal or savory snack while touring the seaside town.

The gastronomic tour of Tamil Nadu is more than simply food; it's a celebration of sensations that dance on the tongue as well as an investigation of cultural intricacies and regional variety. Every dish, from the flavorful kothu parotta, enjoyed beneath the twilight sky to the fragrant filter coffee that begins the day, conveys a tale of love, tradition, and the distinct individuality of Tamil Nadu's culinary legacy. Allow the harmony of spices and the warmth of welcome to lead you on a culinary journey unlike any other as you make your way through the busy streets and traditional restaurants.

PRACTICAL TRAVEL TIPS FOR EXPLORING TAMIL NADU: A Guide to Seamless Exploration

Traveling to Tamil Nadu, the historical and cultural center of South India, requires a balance between readiness and curiosity. From navigating busy streets to indulging in regional specialties, useful travel advice might improve your trip to this energetic state. Let's examine some crucial tips for getting about and having a fulfilling experience in Tamil Nadu, including lodging, banking, language, and transportation.

Transportation Options:

Local Trains and Buses: Traveling between cities and taking in the state's varied landscapes is made easier by Tamil Nadu's vast network of local trains and buses. Trains link major cities and provide beautiful scenery on the way, making them a convenient and reasonably priced choice. The Tamil Nadu State Transport Corporation **(TNSTC)** runs state-owned buses that are an affordable way to travel across small and large distances.

Taxis And Auto Rickshaws: For short trips within cities, auto rickshaws are a well-liked and reasonably priced form of transportation. Before beginning the trip, be sure the driver agrees on a fee or utilizes the meter. In cities, taxis are widely accessible and may be booked for day tours or longer excursions. To ensure transparency, haggle over the price in advance or insist on utilizing the meter.

Renting a Vehicle: Renting a vehicle or scooter is an alternative for those who want itinerary flexibility. Major cities have a large number of rental agencies. Particularly in rural locations, be informed about local traffic laws and road conditions. For overseas visitors, having a current international driving permit is advised.

Mobile Ride-Sharing Apps: In cities like Chennai, ride-sharing applications like Ola and Uber are extensively used. With transparent pricing and a cashless payment method, these applications provide a dependable and easy way to schedule rides. To use apps seamlessly, make sure your mobile data is activated.

Accommodation Recommendations:

Cost-effective Accommodations: Tamil Nadu has a selection of lodging choices to suit a variety of budgets. In both urban and rural locations, tourists on a tight budget may check out guesthouses, hostels, and inexpensive hotels. Clean and reasonably priced rooms are offered by several government-run guest houses, particularly in well-known tourist locations.

Historical Stays: Especially in areas like Chettinad, choose a historical stay to fully immerse yourself in Tamil Nadu's cultural legacy. Numerous stately residences have been transformed into guesthouses, providing a distinctive and genuine experience.

Online Booking Platforms: To find a range of lodging alternatives, use online booking platforms such as Booking.com, Airbnb, and MakeMyTrip. By offering user evaluations, these services help you make well-informed selections by drawing on the experiences of other travelers.

Make Reservations in Advance: Accommodations tend to fill up fast during popular travel seasons or big events. Reservations should be made well in advance, particularly for well-known locations like Ooty, Kodaikanal, and Mahabalipuram.

Communication and Language:

Tamil Language: Although the state's official language is Tamil, English is often used among younger people, in metropolitan areas, and tourist spots. Nonetheless, you may show respect for local culture and improve your contacts with them by picking up a few simple Tamil words.

Translation programs: You should think about using translation programs like Google Translate to overcome linguistic hurdles. With the aid of these applications, you may interact with non-English speakers and read Tamil menus and signage.

Cultural Sensitivity: People from Tamil Nadu value tourists who respect their traditions and customs since the state has a rich cultural past. Sayings like "Nandri" (thank you) and "Vanakkam" (hello) may greatly enhance constructive relationships.

Currency and Banking:

Indian Rupee (INR): The Indian Rupee is the country's official currency. Make sure you have enough cash, particularly in rural locations where there may be restricted acceptance of credit or debit cards.

ATMs: Major credit/debit cards are accepted in hotels, restaurants, and bigger enterprises, and ATMs are commonly accessible in metropolitan areas. To prevent any problems with using your card, let your bank know about your trip schedule.

Currency Exchange: Major cities and airports provide currency exchange services. To get the most for your money when converting currencies, it's a good idea to evaluate rates and costs beforehand.

Online Banking: You can easily pay bills, transfer money, and keep an eye on your accounts using online banking services. Notify your bank of your trip schedule to prevent any interruptions to your account access.

Extra Advice:

Weather Considerations: The climate of Tamil Nadu is varied, with tropical temperatures found in coastal regions and moderate temperatures found in hill stations. Before your journey, check the weather so that you can pack appropriately.

Cultural etiquette: Dress modestly and take off your shoes before entering temples and other places of worship. In certain places, it is usual to get permission before shooting pictures.

Local Cuisine: Savor Tamil Nadu's delectable cuisine, but exercise caution if your stomach is sensitive. Choose freshly prepared meals from reliable restaurants and stay away from tap water. There's always bottled water accessible.

Health precautions: Bring bug repellent, a basic first aid kit, and any prescription drugs that may be required. Drink plenty of water, particularly when it's hot and muggy outside.

Local Events and Festivals: Before making travel plans, consult the calendar of local events and festivals. Attending festivals may provide special insights into local cultures, but it's important to be mindful of possible crowds and the demand for lodging during these periods.

To sum up, traveling across Tamil Nadu is an enthralling experience full of gastronomic pleasures and cultural discoveries. You may successfully explore the varied landscapes, interact with local customs, and make treasured memories of your South Indian vacation by implementing these useful travel suggestions into your itinerary. The beauty of Tamil Nadu welcomes visitors with open arms and a wealth of activities, whether they want to explore historic temples or indulge in street cuisine.

OFF THE BEATEN PATH IN TAMIL NADU:
Discovering Hidden Gems

Beyond its well-known attractions, Tamil Nadu is a region rich in culture and history. Exploring the unconventional areas of this South Indian state reveals undiscovered treasures that provide genuine interactions, cultural diversity, and a unique viewpoint on the area. These hidden gems provide a window into the spirit of Tamil Nadu, ranging from undiscovered villages to obscure temples and distinctive cultural encounters.

Uncharted Towns:

Kanadukathan in Chettinad: Known for its lavish palaces and majestic residences, Kanadukathan is a hidden treasure nestled in the center of the district. Take a leisurely walk around the peaceful streets and marvel at the architectural splendor of these historic buildings, which include elaborate woodwork, Belgian glass windows, and Italian tiles. Talk to the people to hear the stories behind these impressive homes and learn about Chettinad's rich history.

Poombarai Village near Kodaikanal: Poombarai Village near Kodaikanal calls to those looking for peace and breathtaking scenery. This town, surrounded by terraced fields and lush vegetation, provides a tranquil haven. See the temple in Poombarai village, renowned for its distinctive design and expansive vistas of the Western Ghats. Poombarai's natural beauty is still relatively undisturbed, offering it a paradise for nature lovers and those looking for beautiful surroundings.

Manapad Fishing Village: Tucked away along Tamil Nadu's coastline, this gem of the sea is often overlooked. This charming town is located far from the major tourist attractions and has a stunning coastline and a thriving fishing community. The settlement of Manapad gains historical significance from the 16th-century St. James Church. Take in the simplicity of this undiscovered seaside hideaway while seeing the fishing community's everyday activities.

Lesser-Known Temples :

Kumbakonam's Adi Kumbeswarar Temple is well-known for its temples, yet it often gets eclipsed by its more well-known peers. This historic temple to Lord Shiva has elaborate architecture as well as a hallowed tank. For those looking for a more private and intimate religious experience, the temple's spiritual atmosphere and historical importance provide a more serene and less crowded option.

Ratnagiri Murugan Temple, Vellore: Perched on a hilltop close to Vellore, the Ratnagiri Murugan Temple is a hidden treasure that offers spiritual seekers a tranquil and expansive environment. The Lord Murugan temple has serene surroundings, a sanctuary resembling a cave, and vibrant sculptures. The temple is a worthwhile and little-visited pilgrimage destination because of the amazing views of the surroundings that come with the ascent to the temple.

Chennai's Thiruvottiyur Thyagaraja Temple provides a tranquil haven despite the city's famously hectic atmosphere. This temple, which honors Lord Shiva, has peacefulness and old architecture. This temple is special because of its connection to the Sage Valmiki tale, which lends a mythological element to the whole spiritual atmosphere.

Distinct Cultural Experiences:

Sivaganga region Ayyanar temples: Explore the Sivaganga region and take in the colorful Ayyanar temples dotted around the rural area. These unusual temples honor the folk god Ayyanar, who is connected to fertility and protection. The Ayyanar temples, adorned with vibrant idols and ceramic horses, provide a glimpse into the customs and beliefs of the surrounding people.

Mamallapuram's Silappathikara Art Village provides a unique cultural experience, despite the city being well-known for its UNESCO-listed structures. The goal of this hamlet is to promote and preserve indigenous Tamil art forms. Witness the creation of elaborate stone sculptures, traditional paintings, and other indigenous crafts by skilled artists. Interact with the artists to learn about Tamil Nadu's rich creative legacy, and consider taking up one of these age-old skills yourself.

Discover the little-known hamlet of Mayiladuthurai, home to a vibrant brass industry that has been sustaining generations of people. Watch how deft craftspeople painstakingly create elaborate brass lamps, utensils, and gods. Talk to the artisans to discover the ancient methods that have been handed down through the ages. Investing in brassware offers a unique keepsake of Tamil Nadu's cultural history and promotes local artisans.

Useful Hints for Discovering Undiscovered Gems:

Local Guides: To find these hidden jewels, hire local guides or ask for advice. Their expertise and insights may deepen your investigation and guarantee that you don't pass up special opportunities.

Respect Local Customs: Be mindful of and mindful of the customs and traditions of the communities and temples you visit. Wear modest clothing, get permission before taking pictures, and abide by any community rules that may be in place.

Flexible plan: Allow for impromptu discoveries by including flexibility into your plan. It's common to find hidden jewels when you stray off the usual route without strict intentions.

Local Transportation: To get about smaller towns and villages, embrace local transportation options like bicycle rickshaws and shared cars. This helps locals sustain their livelihoods while also enhancing their cultural experience.

Off-Peak Visits: If you want to have a more private and tranquil experience, think about going to these hidden jewels during off-peak seasons. This guarantees a more genuine experience and lessens the effect on nearby communities.

Adventuresome tourists are drawn to Tamil Nadu's hidden treasures because they provide a chance to experience the region's spirit, undiscovered history, and rich cultural diversity. These hidden gems highlight the ageless appeal and genuineness that characterize Tamil Nadu's cultural environment, whether you want to explore undiscovered villages, marvel at obscure temples, or partake in unusual cultural events.

RESPONSIBLE TRAVEL IN TAMIL NADU:
Nurturing Nature, Empowering Communities

The values of responsible travel take center stage as visitors set off on the enthralling adventure across Tamil Nadu's varied landscapes and cultural tapestry. Tamil Nadu, a state dedicated to protecting its natural beauty and improving the lives of its people, welcomes exploration with a seamless fusion of historic customs and natural beauties. Traveling responsibly in Tamil Nadu may be a life-changing and sustainable experience by adopting eco-friendly habits, promoting cultural awareness, and helping to save animals.

Eco-Friendly Practices:

Sustainable Accommodations: Choose lodgings that place a high value on environmentally friendly procedures. In Tamil Nadu, a large number of resorts and guesthouses have implemented sustainable practices, such as trash minimization, water conservation, and energy-saving measures. Look for businesses that have earned certification for their ecological responsibilities.

Reducing, Reusing, Recycling: Adopt the maxim "reduce, reuse, recycle" as you go. Reusable water bottles may help reduce the amount of single-use plastic that is used. Make responsible use of the recycling and composting containers provided for disposing of rubbish. To help you lessen your impact on the environment, choose items that come in minimum packaging.

Walking tours and public transit: Reduce your carbon footprint by using public transportation or going on foot explorations. The cities of Tamil Nadu are well-served by buses and trains, providing a more environmentally friendly means of getting about the city. In addition to having a less negative environmental effect, walking tours provide a more immersive experience that enables you to interact with the local people and find hidden treasures.

Select providers who practice ethical wildlife tourism if your schedule involves encounters with animals. Select sanctuaries and reserves that put the welfare of animals first and support conservation initiatives. Steer clear of activities that contribute to the exploitation of animals or put you in close contact with them.

Cultural Immersion in Nature: Take part in eco-friendly activities to fully appreciate Tamil Nadu's stunning natural surroundings. Investigate nature reserves, participate in tree-planting campaigns, or become involved in neighborhood-based conservation efforts. This helps to ensure the biodiversity of the area is preserved over the long term in addition to allowing you to enjoy it.

Showing Local Communities Respect:

Cultural Sensitivity: The people of Tamil Nadu's everyday lives are intricately entwined with their rich cultural legacy. Dress modestly to show respect for other cultures, especially while visiting places of worship and rural areas. To establish a connection with the people and demonstrate your appreciation for their language and customs, pick up a few simple words in Tamil.

Encourage Local Businesses: You may help the community's economy by encouraging small companies, regional artists, and traditional craftspeople. If you buy mementos from local markets, you may be sure that the towns you visit will profit economically from your purchases. Dine at neighborhood restaurants to experience real food and talk to store owners to discover more about their crafts.

Homestays and Community Tourism: Take into account booking a homestay or taking part in events related to community tourism. This helps local households directly while letting you enjoy the warmth of Tamil Nadu hospitality. Homestays often provide genuine cultural interactions and a window into the host community's everyday life.

Responsible Photography: When shooting pictures of locals, particularly in rural regions, get their permission. Steer clear of invasive photography that might interfere with life's organic flow. Respectfully share your experiences, making sure that communities are portrayed in a way that upholds their cultural integrity.

Take Part in Cultural Events: You should think about joining in the festivities if your visit falls during a local festival or other cultural event. This helps to preserve cultural traditions while also offering a unique and immersive experience. Honor the traditions and rituals connected to these occasions.

Preservation of Wildlife:

Select Responsible Wildlife Experiences: There are many different kinds of wildlife in Tamil Nadu, such as tigers, elephants, and many kinds of birds. When choosing an operator for wildlife excursions, make sure they support conservation initiatives and value ethical methods. Steer clear of endeavors that entail the abuse or exploitation of animals.

Education-Based Projects: Encourage the protection of wildlife by implementing educational projects. Visit reserves and animal sanctuaries that place a high priority on environmental education. Discover the local wildlife, the difficulties facing conservation, and the part that communities play in preserving natural areas.

Contribute to Conservation Projects: The biodiversity of Tamil Nadu is actively being protected by a large number of NGOs and conservation groups. Take into consideration volunteering or making a gift to support these projects. Take part in community-led initiatives to protect and restore natural habitats, such as tree-planting campaigns.

Responsible Birdwatching: For those who love to observe birds, Tamil Nadu is a paradise. Keep a respectful distance from nesting places and refrain from engaging in any activity that can annoy birds as part of responsible birdwatching. Follow responsible birding protocols to reduce your influence on the bird ecology.

Trekking and nature hikes in Tamil Nadu should be done responsibly. Follow these guidelines if you want to experience the state's beautiful scenery in this way. To preserve habitat, refrain from littering, and observe the Leave No Trace philosophy, stay on authorized paths. Observe the advice given by regional authorities and environmental advocacy groups.

To sum up, ethical travel in Tamil Nadu is a dedication to making a beneficial difference for the local community, the environment, and animals. Travelers may make sure that their exploration of Tamil Nadu adheres to sustainability ideals by using eco-friendly habits, honoring local customs, and making contributions to conservation initiatives. Allow your trip to catalyze good change and a celebration of the connectivity of people and the earth while you take in the natural beauty and cultural diversity of the area.

TAMIL NADU: A Tapestry of Experiences for Families and Solo Travelers

With its dynamic culture, age-old customs, and varied scenery, Tamil Nadu provides a wide range of experiences for both single and family visitors. Explore historic temples, indulge in delectable cuisine, or just take in the tranquil surroundings—Tamil Nadu extends a warm welcome to everyone. We'll explore kid-friendly vacation destinations in this guide, as well as advice for single visitors looking to explore the state on their own. We'll also look at how families and lone travelers may interact with the kind people of Tamil Nadu to make their trip there really unforgettable.

Activities Suitable for Families:

Shore Temple and Beach at Mahabalipuram:
Mahabalipuram is a family-friendly treasure trove and a UNESCO World Heritage site. Discover the elaborate stone carvings that tell stories from Hindu mythology at the Shore

Temple, a magnificent example of Dravidian architecture. Following your historical excursion, take the family to a local beach for a leisurely meal while making sandcastles and taking in the soft sea air.

MGM Dizzee World, Chennai: MGM Dizzee World in Chennai is a great place for a fun-filled family adventure day. All age groups may enjoy the wide variety of rides, water attractions, and entertainment acts that this amusement park has to offer. MGM Dizzee World promises an exciting and hilarious day for younger kids with its thrilling roller coasters, water slides, and designated play area.

Ooty's Botanical Gardens and Toy Train Ride: With its gorgeous scenery and enjoyable activities, Ooty's hill station is a family-friendly paradise. Take a trip to the Government Botanical Gardens, where kids may adore an array of unique flowers and plants. Later, take a magnificent journey over the verdant hills on the Nilgiri Mountain Railway, often known as the Toy Train, which offers expansive vistas of the Nilgiris.

Families may find peace in Kodaikanal, sometimes referred to as the Princess of Hill Stations, with its Coaker's Walk and Boat Ride. Enjoy a relaxed walk along the paved

Coaker's Walk, which offers stunning views of the hills in the area. Take a leisurely boat trip on Kodaikanal Lake, where families may paddle together while taking in the beautiful flora and quiet of the lake.

Family Cooking Workshops in Chettinad: Take part in family-friendly cooking workshops to fully immerse your family in the region's culinary tradition. Discover the skill of cooking authentic Chettinad cuisine, including tasty rice dishes and fragrant curries. Along with being a delightful event, it's a chance for the family to become closer to common culinary pursuits.

Solo Travel Tips

Cultural Awareness: Getting fully immersed in the local way of life may greatly enrich the experience of lone travelers visiting Tamil Nadu. Take the effort to learn a few simple Tamil words and show respect for the customs and traditions of the area. Traveling alone is much more enjoyable when interactions with locals are attentive to cultural differences.

Although Tamil Nadu is usually seen to be secure for lone travelers, it is still important to use common sense care. Be mindful of your surroundings, protect your things, and stay away from dimly lit or remote regions, particularly at night. Tell a trusted person about your trip arrangements.

Make Friends with Other Travelers: Meeting other lone explorers may foster a sense of kinship for solo travelers. Social media groups, travel forums, and hostels may all be great places to meet other travelers, exchange stories, and even team up on excursions or activities.

Use Local Transportation: To get about various cities and towns, make use of the local transportation choices that are available, such as buses and trains. In addition to offering a more genuine travel experience, this enables lone travelers to make connections with locals while on the road.

Investigate Off the Beaten Path: Travelers traveling alone have the freedom to discover undiscovered attractions and unusual locations. Explore the less-traveled-to locations to find undiscovered temples, charming towns, and tranquil scenery. Solo excursions are made much more rich by the feeling of discovery.

Getting to Know the Locals:

Homestays and Community Experiences: Selecting a homestay or taking part in a community experience may improve a trip for both families and lone travelers. Intimate glimpses into residents' everyday lives are provided via homestays, which promote cross-cultural dialogue and sincere relationships. Participate in community projects or local festivals to show your support for the community.

Language Learning: By picking up a little Tamil, families and lone tourists may forge closer ties with the people they visit. When it comes to overcoming language difficulties and getting kind replies from locals, even simple statements may make a big difference. Studying keywords before and during the journey is made simple by language study applications and internet resources.

Attend Local Events and Festivals: By going to local events and festivals, both families and lone travelers may fully immerse themselves in Tamil Nadu's colorful culture. During these festivities, one may experience the community's joyous celebration while taking in traditional dancing, music, and traditions.

Encourage Local Artists and Marketplaces: By encouraging local craftsmen and marketplaces, families and lone tourists may help the community's economy. Buy directly from artists to ensure that the creators get the money they deserve for their handcrafted goods, linens, and mementos. Talking with craftspeople will offer you an understanding of their work and customs.

Take Part in Cultural Workshops: By taking part in cultural workshops, families may add an engaging and informative element to their trip. These fascinating activities provide children and adults with an opportunity to learn about the rich cultural history of Tamil Nadu, ranging from traditional arts and crafts sessions to music and dance workshops.

In summary, Tamil Nadu proves to be a flexible vacation location that meets the various requirements of both single and family visitors. The state provides a variety of experiences, whether traveling to family-friendly sights, navigating excursions by yourself, or making connections with welcoming people. Tamil Nadu is a monument to the friendliness and inclusiveness that characterize South India's culture, as families forge enduring memories and lone travelers set off on life-changing adventures.

BEYOND TAMIL NADU: Exploring Nearby Destinations

While the rich legacy and varied landscapes of Tamil Nadu enthrall, the surrounding areas provide a tapestry of experiences that balance the state's cultural charm. Explore the captivating charm of Pondicherry, the tranquil backwaters of Kerala, and the temple towns and gardens of Karnataka by venturing beyond the boundaries of Tamil Nadu.

Pondicherry, A French Affair:

Pondicherry, a seaside town on Tamil Nadu's northern border, entices with its distinct fusion of French and Indian elements. Pondicherry, a former French colony, has a certain beauty that comes from its colonial architecture, boulevards lined with trees, and peaceful shoreline.

Explore the French Quarter: Take a stroll through the charming French Quarter, often called the White Town, where buildings from the colonial period transport tourists back in time. A charming scene is created by the vivid hues of the homes, which are complemented by wrought-iron balconies and bougainvillea. See famous sites that showcase Pondicherry's French legacy, such as the Basilica of the Sacred Heart of Jesus and the Notre Dame des Anges.

Auroville, often known as the City of Dawn, is an experimental community located not far from Pondicherry that exists outside of national borders. Auroville was founded on the idea of human togetherness, and the Matrimandir—a golden globe that represents the town—is located there. Explore the Matrimandir Gardens and join meditation classes to feel the peace that this special community exudes.

Promenade Beach: Relax at this lovely length of beach where the Bay of Bengal washes softly against the coast. The lively street markets and cafés along the promenade make it the perfect place for people to unwind by the sea or take strolls. The beach becomes a mystical place for an evening stroll when the sun sets.

Kerala: Backwaters and Beyond

Travel from Tamil Nadu to Kerala, a state known for its beautiful scenery, serene backwaters, and rich cultural history. Kerala offers an intriguing contrast to Tamil Nadu with its varied attractions, which include houseboat cruises and old temples.

Backwater Houseboat Cruises: Travel through the tranquil network of canals and lagoons that make up Kerala's backwaters. Houseboat trips provide an exceptional viewpoint of the verdant surroundings, charming towns, and customary lifestyle along the rivers. Often used as the beginning places for these immersion adventures are Alleppey and Kumarakom.

Discover **Kochi**, a city that perfectly captures the fusion of many cultures and traditions, via its Cultural Tapestry. The famous Chinese fishing nets, colonial buildings, and historic churches highlight the Fort Kochi neighborhood. Explore the Jewish synagogue and take in the lively ambiance of the antique stores as you visit Jew Town.

Periyar National Park: Known for its lush woods and variety of species, Periyar National Park is located in Thekkady and is a great destination for nature lovers. To see elephants, deer, and a variety of bird species in their natural environment, go on a boat safari on Periyar Lake. Those looking for a closer experience with nature may also go hiking in the park.

Karnataka: Gardens and Temple Towns

Karnataka, a state with a rich historical and cultural past, is located northwest of Tamil Nadu. Karnataka provides a wide range of experiences, from the historic temples of Hampi to the well-maintained gardens of Bangalore.

The Archaeological Wonders of Hampi: An outdoor museum of ancient ruins and temples, Hampi is a UNESCO World Heritage site. The ancient capital of the Vijayanagara Empire, Hampi, is home to magnificent temples, ornate stone sculptures, and the famous Virupaksha Temple. Boulder-studded, bizarre scenery makes for an enthralling background for exploring.

The Royal Heritage of Mysuru: Mysuru, also known as Mysore, is renowned for its opulence and depth of culture. The Mysuru Palace entices guests with its sumptuous interiors and immaculate grounds, making it a magnificent example of Indo-Saracenic architecture. Savor the city's renowned Mysore Pak, a delicious treat, and explore the lively Devaraja Market.

Bangalore's Gardens and Tech Hub: The dynamic metropolis of Bangalore skillfully combines modern technology with a backdrop of breathtaking scenery. One of the city's treasures, Lalbagh Botanical Garden, is home to the famous Glass House and an amazing collection of exotic plants. Bangalore is home to a dynamic food culture, vibrant street markets, and art galleries alongside a burgeoning IT environment.

To sum up, venturing outside of Tamil Nadu reveals an abundance of diverse experiences, with every nearby location presenting a unique character and cultural fabric. The peaceful backwaters of Kerala, the French elegance of Pondicherry, and the temple towns of Karnataka come together to form a harmonic whole that accentuates the historical and scenic beauties of Tamil Nadu. Whether you're looking for peace, cultural discovery, or architectural wonders, the neighboring areas enrich and diversify the travel experiences offered by South India.

CONCLUSION

To sum up, Tamil Nadu is a complex treasure that welcomes visitors to a world where vibrant metropolitan landscapes combine with age-old customs. Tamil Nadu has a story spanning centuries, from the architectural wonders of Chennai to the serene beaches, lush hill stations, and temple cities. The state's vibrant culture, which is shown in its dance, music, and culinary offerings, provides visitors with a feast for the senses.

Tamil Nadu's warmth and variety make a lasting impression on families creating enduring memories and lone travelers setting off on life-changing adventures. Beyond its boundaries, Kerala, Karnataka, and Pondicherry beckon with their own stories that weave more threads into the fabric of South India. The real warmth of Tamil Nadu's people, along with the state's rich historical legacy, make every visit a voyage into the soul of this enthralling southern region.

EPILOGUE: Unveiling Hidden Legends - Untold Stories of Tamil Nadu

Discover the unseen tales and obscure legends that have influenced the cultural fabric of this remarkable state as you delve deeper into Tamil Nadu with this special additional chapter that goes beyond the mainstream narratives. Learn the stories behind historic temples, timeless legends, and undiscovered treasures that are often missed by conventional travel guides.

Temple Mysteries: Discover the secrets kept within Tamil Nadu's well-known temples. This part takes readers on a mystical trip, exposing the lesser-known facets of these treasured sanctuaries, from the fascinating architectural mysteries to the holy rites that transcend time.

Folktales and Fables: Get lost in the intricate web of folktales and fables from Tamil Nadu. These engrossing tales, handed down over the ages, provide a unique perspective on the regional culture. Examine the entrancing stories, moral teachings, and symbols that people still find meaningful in their everyday lives.

Undiscovered Routes and Hikes: Explore off-the-beaten paths with our comprehensive guides to undiscovered routes and hikes that highlight Tamil Nadu's varied topography. This area encourages readers to go on adventures that provide seclusion, breathtaking scenery, and a closer connection with the natural world. These excursions range from remote nature reserves to expansive views.

Culinary Chronicles: Savor Tamil Nadu's delectable cuisine by delving deeper into the state's delicacies, uncovering the mysteries of street food, and learning the backstories of its tastes. Enticing readers to enjoy the spirit of Tamil Nadu via its rich palette, this chapter offers an intimate tour of the state's culinary gems, from the busy marketplaces to family kitchens.

Living Traditions: Explore Tamil Nadu's living traditions with in-depth segments on modern dance, music, and art. See how classical art forms have evolved, meet the keepers of age-old crafts, and discover how modernity and tradition combine to create a dynamic and ever-changing cultural environment.

With the help of this additional chapter, the reader's trip is elevated from a simple investigation to a genuine voyage, providing a thorough and immersive understanding of Tamil Nadu's natural, historical, and cultural treasures. It serves as a passport to the unusual, guaranteeing that each page flipped will unveil a fresh dimension of the state's enchantment. Take an incredible journey with the mysteries and surprises that Tamil Nadu has kept solely for those who dare to seek them out. Don't simply travel.

Printed in Great Britain
by Amazon

46349949R00053